CONTENTS

Words in the glossary appear in **bold** type the first time they are used in the text.

MESSI IN MIAMI

Miami is home to many famous people—but few as world-famous as Lionel Messi. Today's biggest soccer star, Messi may be the best soccer player *ever*.

In 2022, Messi helped his country, Argentina, win the World Cup, soccer's biggest worldwide event. In 2023, he joined Miami's Major League Soccer (MLS) team and won his eighth Ballon d'Or, the award for the world's best male soccer player of the year. It was the first time an MLS player won it. Read on to find out more about Messi and other amazing soccer stars.

Get the Stats!

In this book, you'll see FC before and after many teams' names. That stands for Football Club or Futbol Club. In most parts of the world, soccer is called football. (Fútbol is Spanish for football.)

Sports Stars, Stats, and Stories

SOCCER STARS, STATS, AND STORIES

BY TY SCHALTER

Enslow PUBLISHING

INVESTIGATE!

Please visit our website, www.enslow.com. For a free color catalog of all our high-quality books, call toll free 1-800-398-2504 or fax 1-877-980-4454.

Cataloging-in-Publication Data
Names: Schalter, Ty.
Title: Soccer stars, stats, and stories / Ty Schalter.
Description: Buffalo, NY : Enslow Publishing, 2025. | Series: Sports stars, stats, and stories| Includes glossary and index.
Identifiers: ISBN 9781978542631 (pbk.) | ISBN 9781978542648 (library bound) | ISBN 9781978542655 (ebook)
Subjects: LCSH: Soccer–History–Juvenile literature. | Soccer teams–Anecdotes–Juvenile literature. | Soccer players–Juvenile literature. | Soccer–Statistical methods–Juvenile literature.
Classification: LCC GV943.25 S33 2025 | DDC 796.334–dc23

Published in 2025 by
Enslow Publishing
2544 Clinton Street
Buffalo, NY 14224

First Edition

Designer: Andrea Davison-Bartolotta
Editor: Therese Shea

Photo credits: Cover, pp. 1 (Alex Morgan), 17 (bottom), 19 (bottom) lev radin/Shutterstock.com; cover (ball) DenisNata/Shutterstock.com; cover (cards) Kirill Kurashov/Shutterstock.com; cover, p. 1 (cone) Mboisker Creative/Shutterstock.com; cover, p. 1 (field) Vitalii Vitleo/Shutterstock.com; cover, p. 1 (game plan) PeopleImages.com - Yuri A/Shutterstock.com; series art (banners) WinWin artlab/Shutterstock.com; series art (jersey texture) Kwangmoozaa/Shutterstock.com; series art (fact box background) Igor Link/Shutterstock.com; series art (tablet) Lemberg Vector studio/Shutterstock.com; p. 5 Ringo Chiu/Shutterstock.com; pp. 6, 7 A.RICARDO/Shutterstock.com; p. 9 (Messi) Fabideciria/Shutterstock.com; p. 9 (Ronaldo) Stefan Constantin 22/Shutterstock.com; p. 9 (header) Theme Peek/Shutterstock.com; p. 11 (map) PorcupenWorks/Shutterstock.com; p. 11 (right) Christian Bertrand/Shutterstock.com; p. 11 (left) Natursports/Shutterstock.com; p. 12 Cesar Ortiz Gonzalez/Shutterstock.com; p. 13 (left) Marta Fernandez Jimenez/Shutterstock.com; p. 13 (right) Victor Velter/Shutterstock.com; pp. 14, 15 (bottom) ph.FAB/Shutterstock.com; p. 15 (DeBruyne) Vitalii Vitleo/Shutterstock.com; p. 15 (Erling, Rodrigo) Ververidis Vasilis/Shutterstock.com; p. 17 (top) Jose Breton- Pics Action/Shutterstock.com; p. 18 Keeton Gale/Shutterstock.com; p. 19 (top) Amin Monfared/Shutterstock.com; p. 20 Emanuele Nocerino/Shutterstock.com; p. 21 Aflo Co. Ltd./Alamy Stock Photo; p. 22 (Ferguson) photoyh/Shutterstock.com; p. 22 (Klopp) Oleksandr Osipov/Shutterstock.com; p. 23 (logos) Julia Babii/Shutterstock.com; p. 23 (main) mooinblack/Shutterstock.com; p. 25 (bottom left) Verhoeff, Bert/Anefo photo collection/Netherland National Archives, CC0; p. 25 (bottom right) Crown, Ron/Anefo photo collection/Netherland National Archives, CC0; p. 25 (top) Paolo Bona/Shutterstock.com; p. 26 Photo Works/Shutterstock.com; p. 27 (top) Daniel Motz/Alamy Stock Photo; p. 27 (trophy) fifg/Shutterstock.com; p. 28 Hasan Shaheed/Shutterstock.com; p. 29 (bottom left) FamVeld/Shutterstock.com; p. 29 (bottom right) andres barrionuevo lopez/Shutterstock.com; p. 29 (top) Photo Works/Shutterstock.com.

Printed in the United States of America

CPSIA compliance information: Batch #CW25ENS: For further information contact Enslow Publishing, at 1-800-398-2504.

Inter Miami FC fans can't get enough of their superstar, Lionel Messi. In 2024, he was the first player in MLS history to make five assists in a single game. An assist is a pass that leads to a goal.

BRAZIL'S BEST

Edson Arantes do Nascimento, better known as Pelé, was the world's first soccer superstar. Pelé led Brazil to three World Cup wins (1958, 1962, and 1970). He's the only player to do that. He played for the New York Cosmos in the 1970s too. His skill and style made millions love the sport.

Marta Vieira da Silva, known as just "Marta," has scored more World Cup goals for Brazil than Pelé. Her 17 World Cup goals are the most ever! She also is the Brazil national team's leading goal scorer with 118. Marta is captain of the Orlando Pride of the National Women's Soccer League (NWSL).

PELÉ

Marta has won the FIFA Player of the Year award six times. FIFA stands for Fédération Internationale de Football Association. This organization oversees international, or worldwide, soccer as well as the World Cup.

MARTA

Get the Stats!

*Marta is the only player, man or woman, to score in five different World Cups. She's also the first to score in five **Olympics**.*

WHO'S BETTER: MESSI OR RONALDO?

When Messi was young, he was much smaller than his peers. He had to have growth **hormone** shots. At age 13, he joined Spain's FC Barcelona. He scored 672 goals, breaking Pelé's one-team record. Messi led Barcelona to 10 La Liga league titles.

Cristiano Ronaldo of Portugal has used his speed and powerful shot to score more goals than any other player in men's international soccer—130. He has set records for England's Manchester United FC as well as Spain's Real Madrid CF (Club de Fútbol). For Real Madrid, he scored 451 times in 438 games.

Ronaldo	VS	Messi
5	Ballons d'Or	8
765	club goals	729
216	club assists	319
130	international goals	109
36	international assists	55
7	league titles	12
5	**UEFA Champions League** wins	4
0	World Cup wins	1

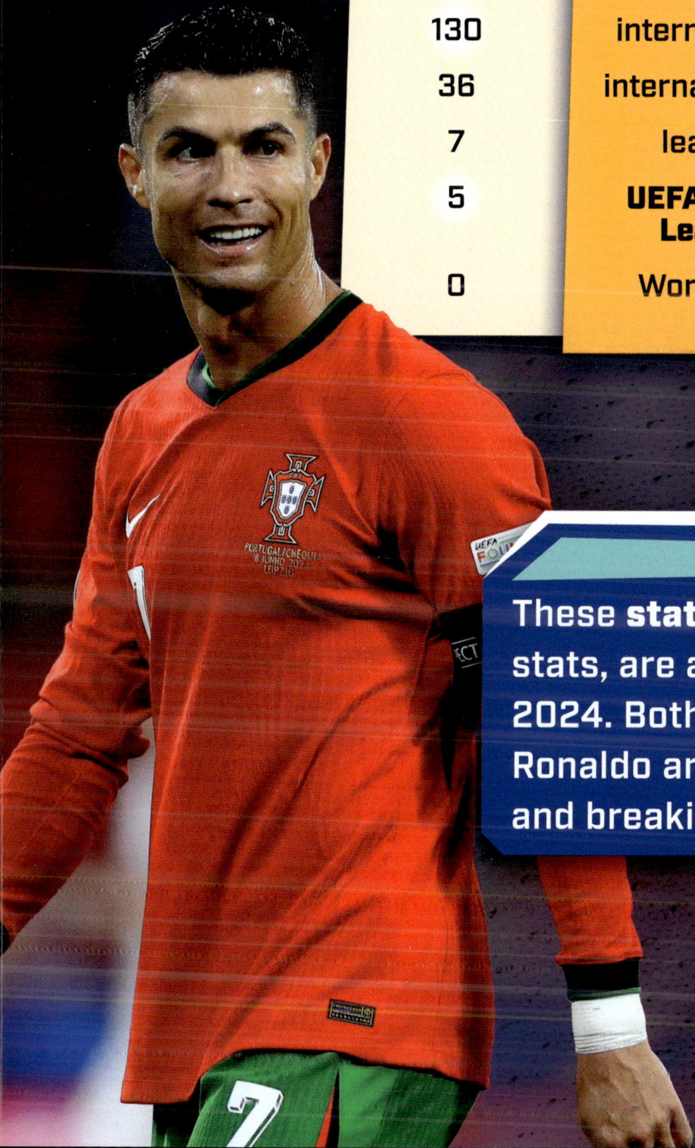

These **statistics**, or stats, are as of July 2024. Both Messi and Ronaldo are still playing and breaking records!

REAL MADRID VS. BARCELONA: EL CLÁSICO

The team FC Barcelona is a source of great pride to the Catalon people in Spain. In 1920, Spain's king gave the team Real Madrid CF its royal title. (*Real* means "royal.") When these two **rivals** play each other, it's called *El Clásico* (The Classic).

In the 2010s, Messi and Ronaldo made El Clásicos a must-watch for soccer fans around the world, including more and more Americans. As of April 2024, Real Madrid has won a few more El Clásicos, 105 to 100.

Get the Stats!

Real Madrid have won more La Liga titles (36) than Barcelona (27).

Messi has the most El Clásico goals of any player with 26. Ronaldo and Alfredo Di Stefano follow with 18 each.

EUROPE'S BIG FIVE

These are the top five European men's soccer leagues in size and popularity.

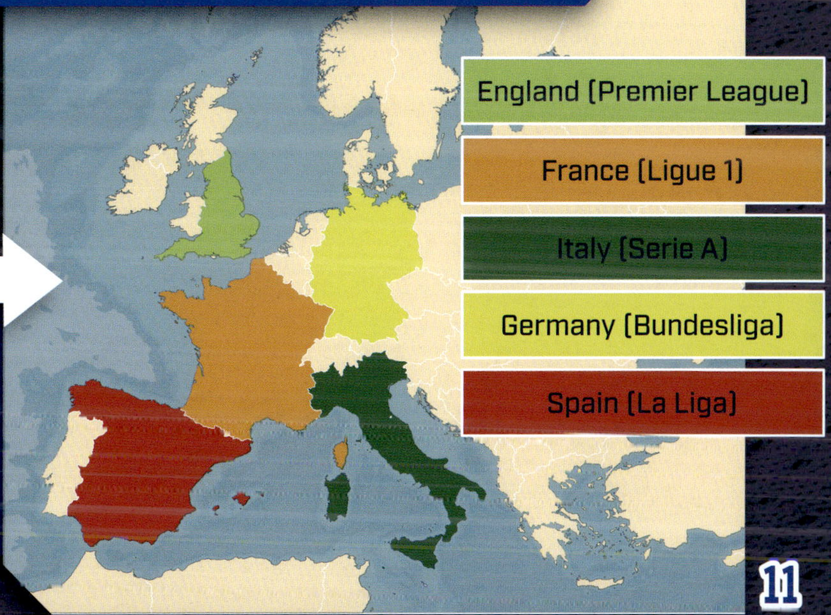

REAL'S RISING STARS

Real Madrid aren't just considered royalty in Spain. They're soccer kings of Europe. They've won the UEFA Champions League a record 15 times as of the 2023-2024 season, aided by Brazil's star **forward** Vini Jr. (Vinícius José Paixão de Oliveira Júnior) and England's exciting **midfielder** Jude Bellingham.

In June 2024, Real Madrid added more speed and power with forward Kylian Mbappé. Mbappé has led France's national team to two straight Men's World Cup finals. France won in 2018 and lost to Messi's Argentinian team in 2022.

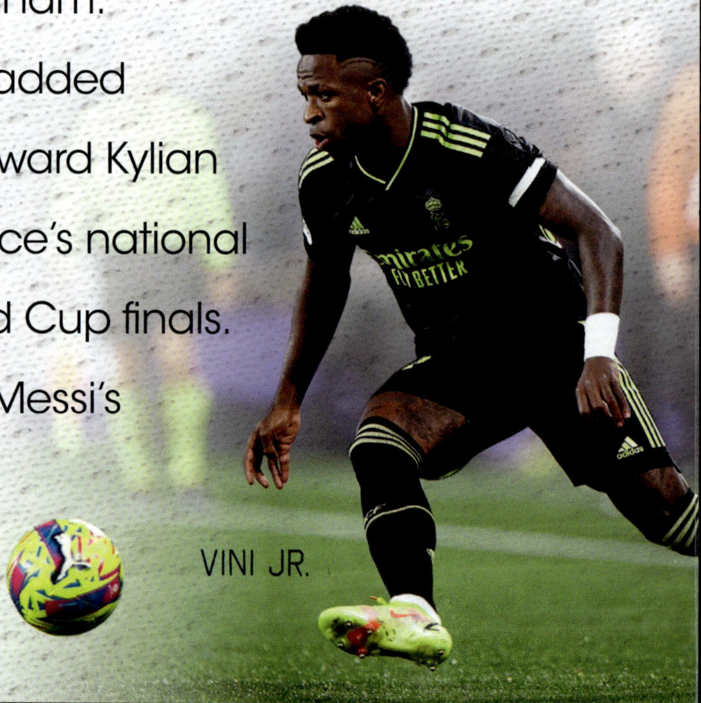

VINI JR.

While playing with Paris Saint-Germain FC, Mbappé was the top scorer of the French soccer league Ligue 1 in 2023-2024, with 27 goals.

MANCHESTER CITY'S THREE GREATS

Alf-Inge Haaland played for Manchester City FC from 2000 to 2003. Twenty years later, in 2023, City signed his son Erling. A large, fast, powerful **striker**, Erling scored 36 times that season, the most goals ever scored in a Premier League season. Manchester City won their first Champions League title in 2023.

Erling plays beside two of the world's best midfielders. Kevin de Bruyne sets up goals, while Rodrigo Hernández Cascante, known as Rodri or Rodrigo, gets the ball back. All three players finished top five in Ballon d'Or voting for 2023-2024.

Erling Haaland, above, scored 50 goals faster than any Premier League player in 48 games.

BEST EVER, STILL GREAT: THE USWNT

Back when many countries didn't allow women's soccer, U.S. laws made sure women had equal opportunities. That helped the U.S. Women's National Team (USWNT) win the most Women's World Cups (four) and Olympic gold medals (five). Still, for years, they were paid much less than the men's national team. In 2022, they won an equal contract!

Megan Rapinoe was one of the star players who fought for that contract. A USWNT **winger**, Rapinoe won the Women's Ballon d'Or in 2019. She's also well known for speaking out for equal rights.

The USWNT celebrates winning the 2019 Women's World Cup against the Netherlands.

Get the Stats!

Rapinoe is the only player, male or female, to score with a corner kick at the Olympics. This is called an Ollmpico. She's done it twice!

CORNER KICK

A TALE OF TWO THORNS

Christine Sinclair has scored more goals for Canada's national team than any man or woman has for any other country, 190. She also captained the Portland Thorns FC to three National Women's Soccer League (NWSL) titles, in 2013, 2017, and 2022.

The Portland Thorns chose Sophia Smith as their number one pick in 2020. In 2022, the NWSL named Smith the Most Valuable Player after she, Sinclair, and the Thorns won that year's championship. In 2023, Smith led the NWSL in goals (11) and many other stats. Smith also plays with the USWNT.

PORTLAND THORNS GAME

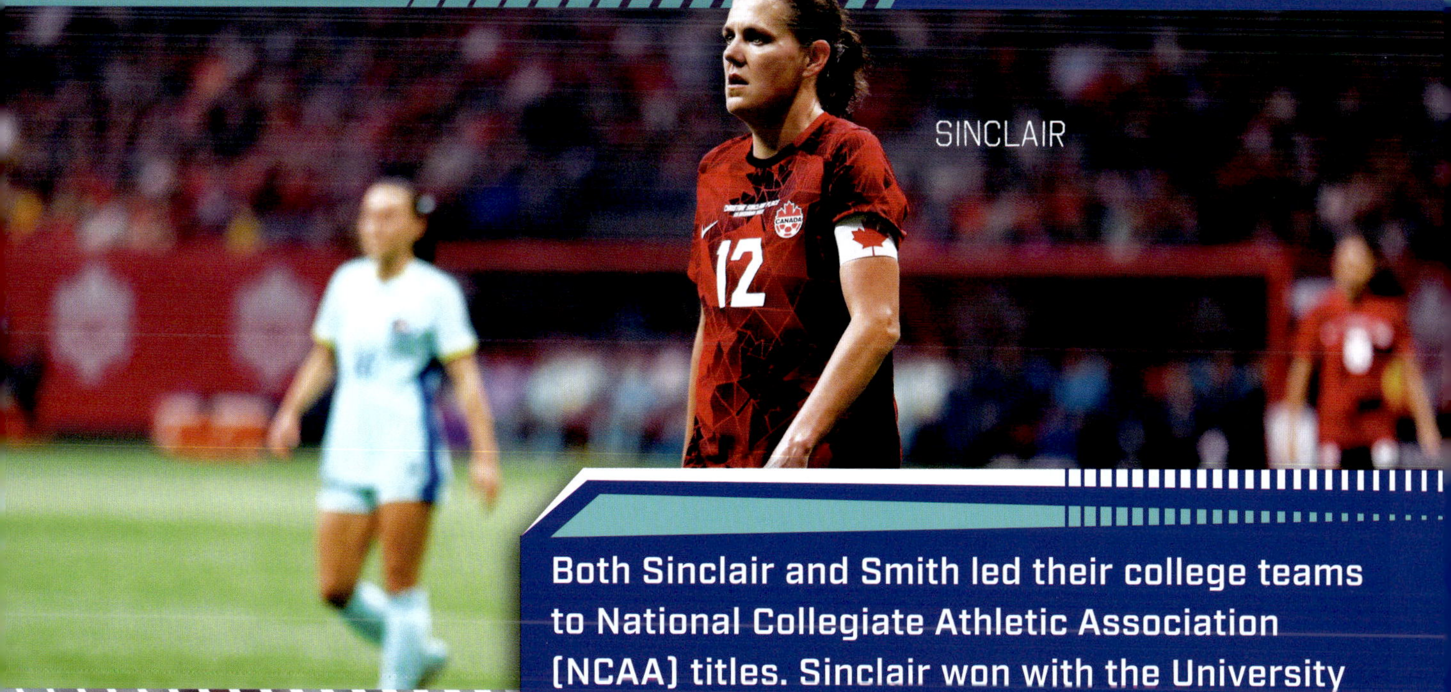

SINCLAIR

Both Sinclair and Smith led their college teams to National Collegiate Athletic Association (NCAA) titles. Sinclair won with the University of Portland Pilots in 2002 and 2005. Smith won with the Stanford Cardinals in 2019.

SMITH

THE GOLDEN BOY

Before Messi, there was Diego Maradona. The short, skilled Argentinian, nicknamed *El Pibe de Oro* (The Golden Boy), won the 1986 World Cup with two amazing goals.

One goal came off his hand, unseen by officials. He later said it was "the hand of God," giving the goal a name still remembered today. For the other goal, he **dribbled** the ball all the way from midfield, through England's defenders, to score. It was named FIFA's Goal of the Century!

1986 WORLD CUP QUARTERFINAL ARGENTINA V. ENGLAND

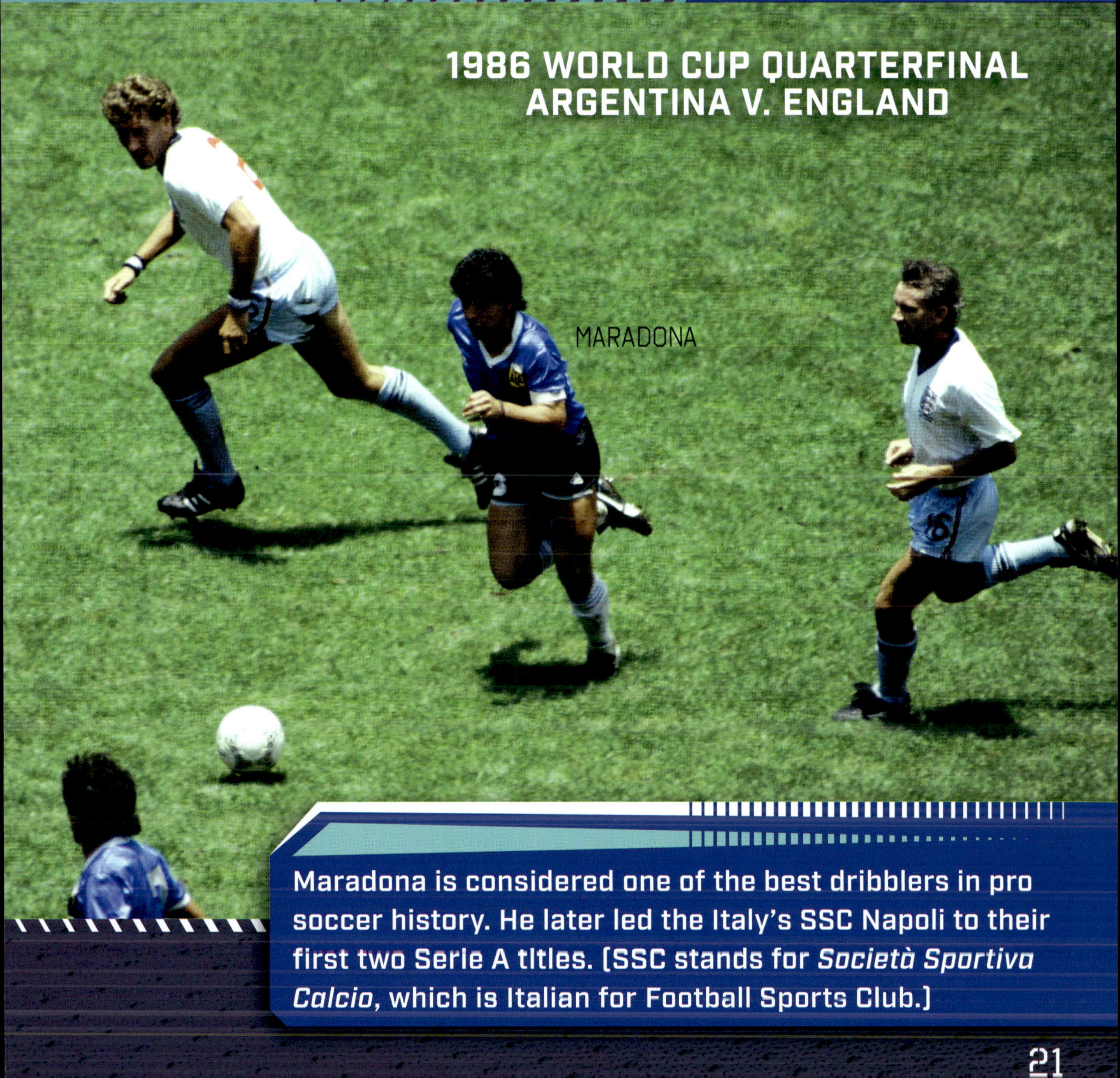

Maradona is considered one of the best dribblers in pro soccer history. He later led the Italy's SSC Napoli to their first two Serie A titles. (SSC stands for *Società Sportiva Calcio*, which is Italian for Football Sports Club.)

THE NORTHWEST DERBY

Manchester United FC and Liverpool FC have closer rivals than each other, but as two of the most successful clubs in the United Kingdom, about 30 miles (48 km) apart, their games are always special.

In the 1960s, they battled for league titles. Beginning in the 1970s, Liverpool took over, winning 11 league titles to United's zero. But then, beginning in the 1990s, **manager** Alex Ferguson led United to 13 titles in 26 years. Liverpool didn't win again until manager Jürgen Klopp put them back on top in 2020.

JÜRGEN KLOPP, ALEX FERGUSON

The Liverpool FC-Manchester United FC rivalry is sometimes called the Northwest Derby. Both cities are in the northwest part of England. In the United Kingdom, a derby is a sports event between teams in the same area.

DOMINANT DUTCH DEFENDER

Virgil van Dijk is a tall, powerful **center back** who began to play for Liverpool in 2018. In 2019, van Dijk finished second in Ballon d'Or voting and became the only defender to win UEFA Men's Player of the Year. How good is he? From March 2018 to August 2019, van Dijk didn't let anyone dribble past him for a record 65 games!

Van Dijk was named captain of the Netherlands national team in 2018. He also served as captain of Liverpool FC for the 2023-2024 season.

Get the Stats!

Another Dutch great, Johan Cruyff, won three Ballons d'Or in the 1970s while playing with Amsterdam Football Club (AFC) Ajax and FC Barcelona. He became a successful manager for Barcelona too.

VAN DIJK

Johan Cruyff, shown in the photos below, is often the first on lists of the best Dutch soccer players. Van Dijk, Edwin van der Sar, Dennis Bergkamp, and Marco van Basten appear on such lists too.

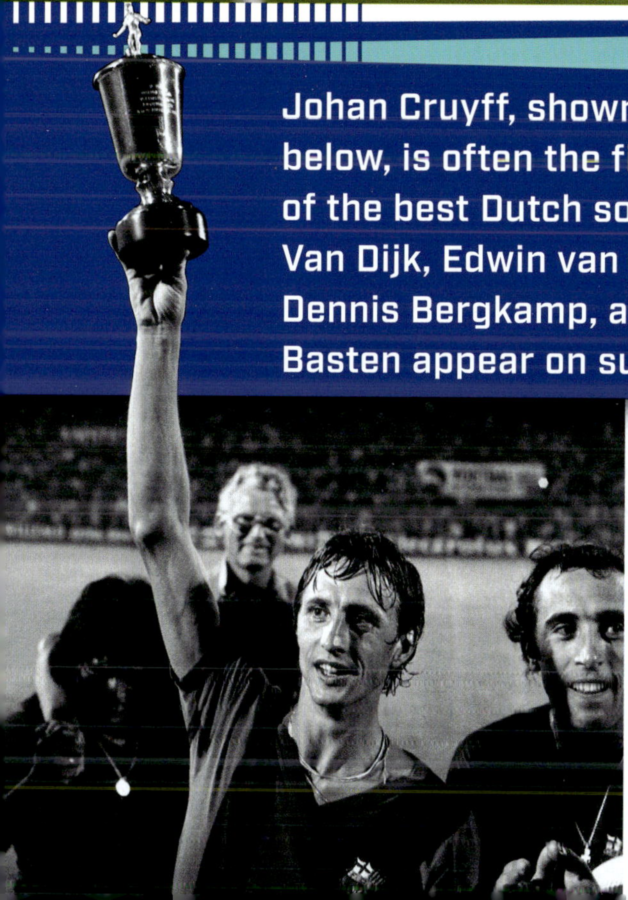

THE U.S. MEN'S NATIONAL TEAM

Perhaps the most important World Cup for the U.S. Men's National Team (USMNT) was in 1994. That year, the United States hosted it. American fans became more interested in the sport at its highest level. Major League Soccer grew out of this World Cup.

The USMNT has made it into the **knockout stage** of the World Cup six times: 1930, 1934, 1994, 2002, 2010, 2014, and 2022. To this day, their third place in 1930 is their best finish. Still, talents such as Landon Donovan, Clint Dempsey, and Tim Howard made more young Americans want to play soccer.

LANDON DONOVAN

USMNT, 2022 WORLD CUP

Get the Stats!

The USMNT didn't make it into the World Cup from 1950 through 1986.

In 2022, the USMNT lost to the Netherlands in the Round of 16. Christian Pulisic, Timothy Weah, and Sergiño Dest, who play for top European clubs, could take the USMNT further in the future.

WORLD CUP TROPHY

DEMERIT'S DETERMINATION

No MLS team wanted Jay DeMerit at first. Still, he believed he could play with the best. He moved to England, playing where he could. Watford FC, a lower-level team, signed him. In 2006, he scored the goal that got Watford into the Premier League! DeMerit played for the USMNT in the 2010 World Cup and captained MLS's Vancouver Whitecaps FC for four seasons.

DeMerit's story shows that Americans can make it in this sport—and make a difference too. Kids playing and watching soccer now are the superstars of tomorrow!

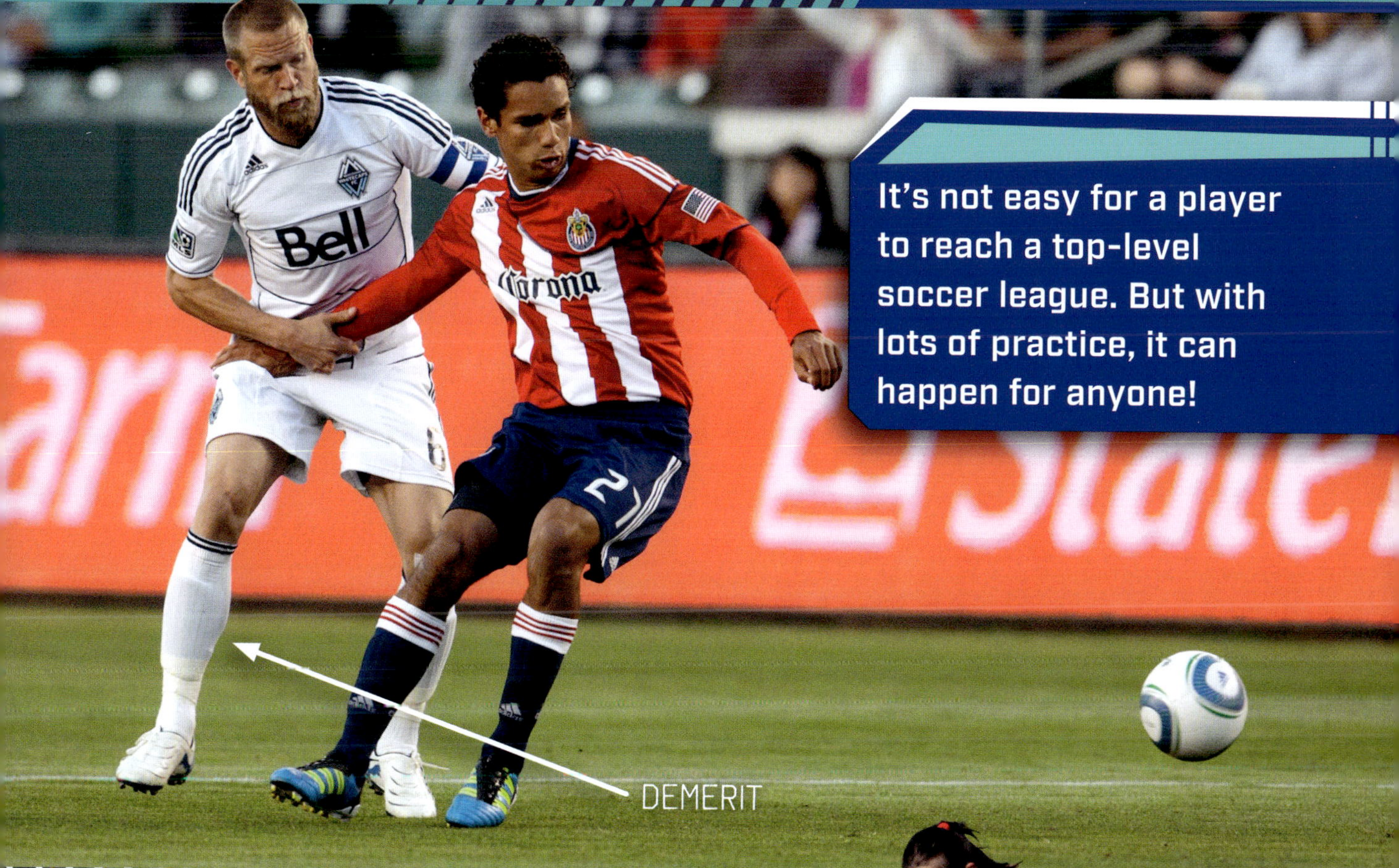

It's not easy for a player to reach a top-level soccer league. But with lots of practice, it can happen for anyone!

GLOSSARY

center back: In soccer, a defender who plays in the center of the field. They protect the goal, block shots, and try to stop the other team's offensive players.

dribble: To advance the ball with taps or bounces with the feet.

forward: In soccer, a player who sets up closer to the opponents' goal and tries to score or assist goals.

hormone: A chemical made in the body that tells another part of the body what to do.

knockout stage: A part of a competition in which the winner of a match advances while the loser is knocked out.

manager: The name for the head coach of a team in many soccer leagues.

midfielder: In soccer, a player who plays defensively and offensively, between the defenders and forwards.

Olympic: Having to do with the Olympic Games, an international sports competition held once every two years, switching between summer and winter games.

rival: A person or group who tries to be more successful than another.

statistics: Information that can be related in numbers. "Stats" is the shortened form.

striker: A forward who plays close to the opponent's goal, in the center of the field.

UEFA Champions League: A season-long tournament of the teams in the Union of European Football Associations (UEFA) that did best in the top European leagues.

winger: In soccer, an attacking player, close to either sideline, who either passes to a striker or takes longer shots.

FOR MORE INFORMATION

BOOKS

Ballheimer, David. *Soccer Legends 2024*. London, UK: Mortimer Children's Limited, 2023.

DK Publishing. *Everything You Need to Know About Soccer!* New York, NY: DK Publishing, 2024.

Gifford, Clive. *The Soccer Encyclopedia*. London, UK: Kingfisher, 2024.

WEBSITES

Football History
www.footballhistory.org
Find lots of great stories about soccer's history, from how it started to today's teams.

Football Statistics and History
fbref.com/en/
Check out stats and rankings for soccer teams and players around the world.

FotMob—Football Live Scores
www.fotmob.com
This site has all the latest scores from games around the world.

Publisher's note to educators and parents: Our editors have carefully reviewed these websites to ensure that they are suitable for students. Many websites change frequently, however, and we cannot guarantee that a site's future contents will continue to meet our high standards of quality and educational value. Be advised that students should be closely supervised whenever they access the Internet.

INDEX